For Belinda, Bob, Anne
and everyone fighting to protect
these animals in their habitat

*A percentage of the royalties from
this book is being donated to the
Wildlife Protection Society of India*

Published by
Mantra Publishing
5 Alexandra Grove
London N12 8NU
www.mantrapublishing.com

Salpicar! Splash!

Flora McDonnell

Portuguese translation by
Emilia Fonseca

mantra

Calor, Calor, Calor!
Os elefantes têm calor.

Hot, hot, hot!
The elephants
are hot.

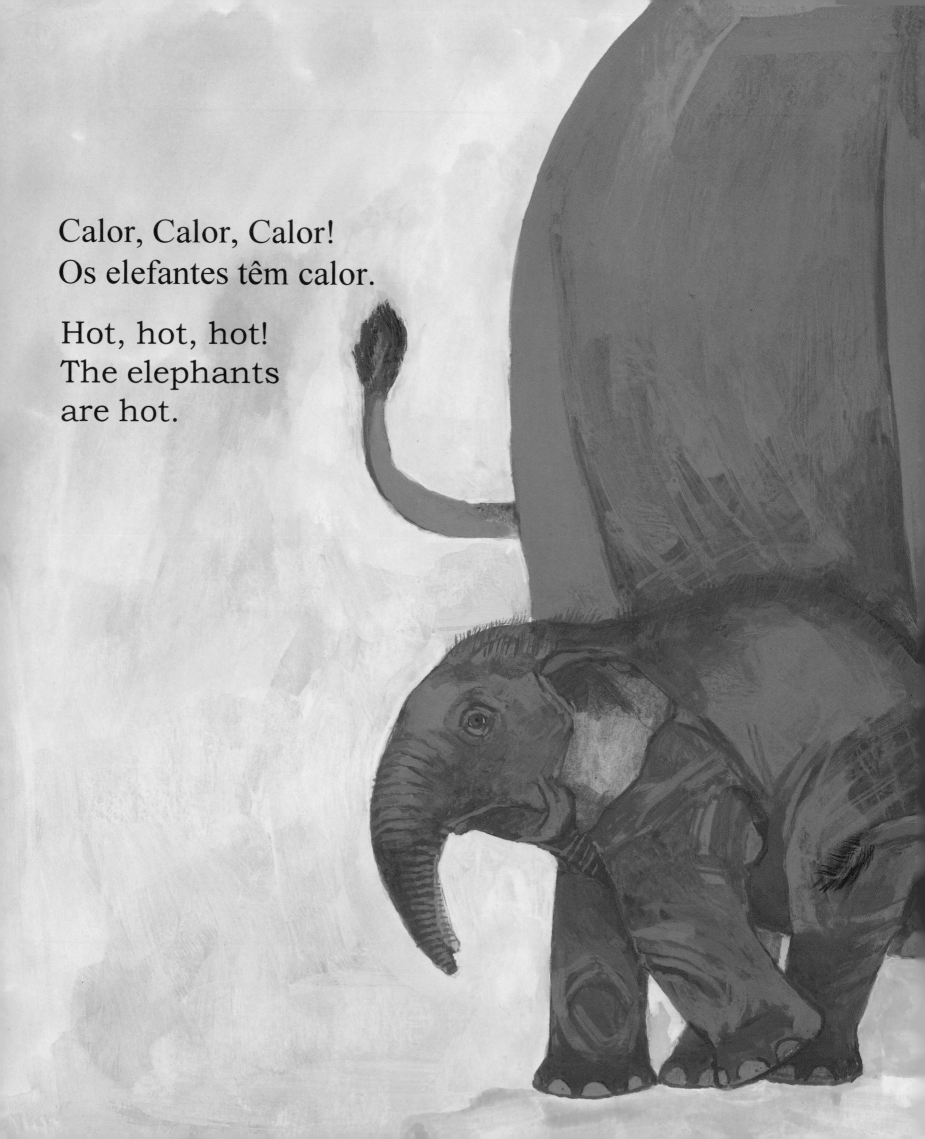

O tigre têm calor.

Tiger is hot.

O rinoceronte têm calor.

Rhinoceros is hot.

Vamos seguir o bébé elefante
até chegar á ...

Let's follow the baby
down to the ...

água, água maravilhosa.

water. Lovely water.

Água para beber.
Água para ...

Water to drink.
Water to ...

squirt,
squirt,
squirt!

Jorrar!
Jorrar!
Jorrar!

Splash!
goes Mother Elephant.

A mãe elefante salpicou!

O rinoceronte salpicou!

Splosh! goes Rhinoceros.

Whoosh!
Sploosh!
goes Tiger.

O tigre
salpicou!

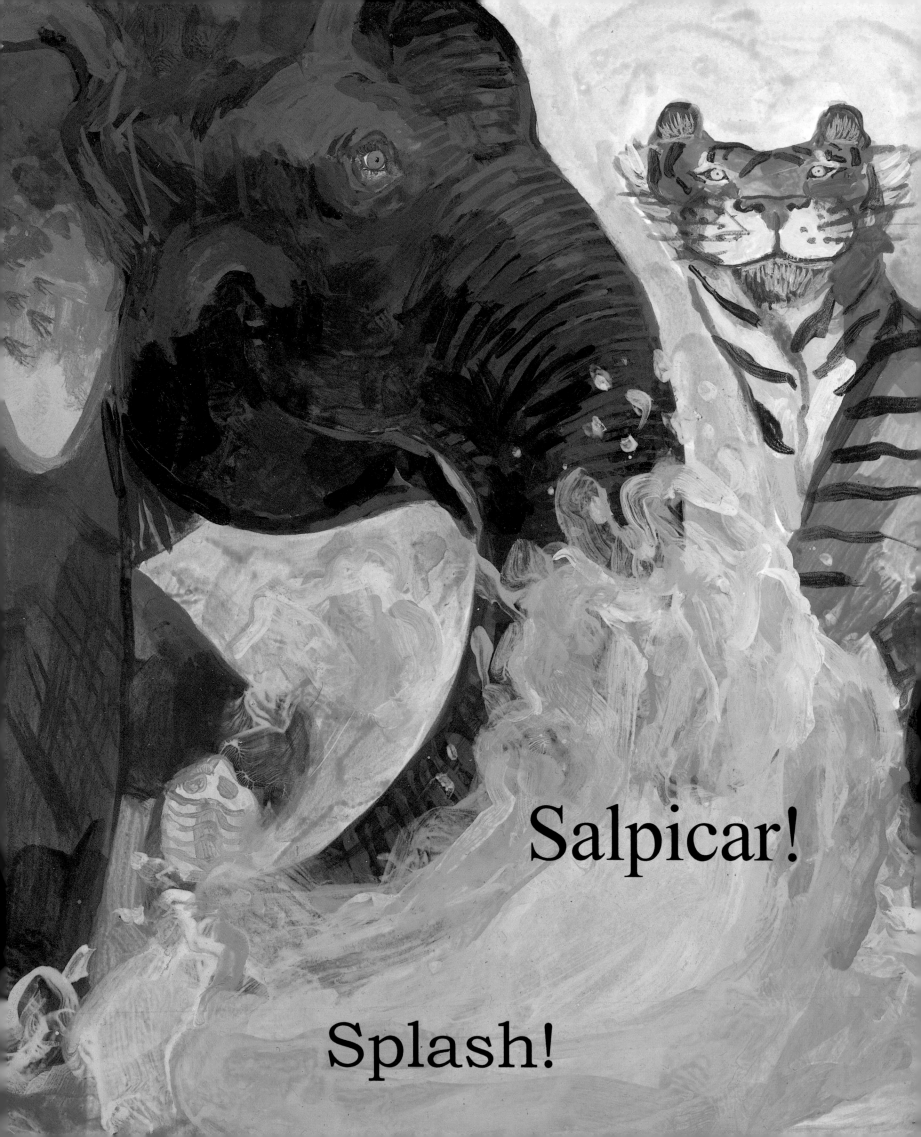

Agora o tigre está
fresco e feliz.

Now Tiger is cool and happy.

Agora o rinoceronte está
fresco e feliz.

Now Rhinoceros is cool and happy.

Agora a mamã
elefante está
fresca e feliz.

Now Mother
Elephant is
cool and happy.

Que contente,
fresco e
inteligente está
o elefante bébé!

What a happy,
cool, clever little
baby elephant!